WENDY ALIDINA

CURRY ON COOKING

*Quick and Tasty Indian
Dishes on a Budget*

To Philippa & Stephen

Lots a love,

Wendy. x

First published in 2010 by The Mayo Press in association with Flare Publications

The Mayo, BCM Box 175, London, WC1X 3XX

Website: www.mayopress.co.uk
Email: contact@mayopress.co.uk

A CIP catalogue record for this book is available from the British Library

ISBN: 978-1-903353-24-0

Publisher's disclaimer: Please note that some recipes include nuts. Please consult your physician for
any allergies or any concerns you may have regarding any ingredients in the following recipes.

Photos taken by Wendy Alidina and Cat Keane

Photo Editing: Terence Goh

Cover: Cat Keane

Layout: Craig Knottenbelt

Text Editing: Heather Knowles

For:
The Alidina Family
Mama, Bapa, Karim, Amin, Shamira,
Salima, Safia, Seline and Zahra

Acknowledgements

Thank you so much to Mama who introduced me to Indian cooking and getting me started.

I would like to extend a very special thank you to Cat Keane for taking several of the photos, cooking some of the recipes with me and testing them, designing the book cover, setting up the website and for making the project so much fun.

I would also like to extend another special thank you to Frank Clifford who guided me through the entire project, editing and advising, encouraging and motivating me.

Also, a big thank you to the following people: Karim Alidina for suggesting the book, Heather Knowles, Emma MacDonald and Frank Clifford for text editing, Terence Goh for his photo editing, Craig Knottenbelt for formatting and layout, Michael Nile for coining the title, Paul Bodimeade, Steve Gawn, Keith Lams, Lilly Walker and Adam White for testing the recipes and all the friends, in particular, Rebecca, Nicky, Shama, Linda and Shirley, who were so helpful and encouraging along the way. Lastly, thank you to my family, Amin, Seline and Zahra who have always been so incredibly supportive.

I couldn't have done it without you all, thank you!

Contents

Introduction

I would be lying if I said that when I married my Muslim Indian husband it wasn't a culture shock. Coming from a diverse background myself, with a culturally wide range of friends and a career working in race relations, I was surprised when confronted with a culture I was unfamiliar with. I found myself stumbling around uncertainly, and I am sure my in-laws experienced something similar. However, while we all found our footing with each other and built relationships, part of that process for me was to spend time with my mother-in-law on her turf, which was her kitchen. I began learning all about what she had absorbed from Indian, African and British influences during varied economic climates and, perhaps most importantly, what she herself had learned from her own mother, aunties, sisters and peers.

During sessions in my mother-in-law's kitchen, I observed and learned from her mastery of combining spices for a variety of dishes using ingredients I had never seen, smelt or tasted before. Today I am still in awe of even how she cuts certain foods and how she makes all the basic ingredients herself – as so many women of her generation do – with an ease and dedication to feed her family and provide enough for those who happen to drop in.

I always used to say that in a previous life I must have been an army cook as the most horrifying thing for me was the thought that there might not be enough food – obviously something I picked up from the older generation. This has always held me in good stead and, of course, makes it possible to really enjoy any leftovers as, when it comes to curries, they always taste better the next day!

No matter how much effort I made, my cooking never seemed to taste like my mother-in-law's. However, over the years I took the knowledge gleaned from her kitchen along with the experience of dining at Indian restaurants – from the authentic and tasty eating places in Southall to fine dining restaurants around the world – and created my own style and taste. **I developed dozens of my own recipes**, which became increasingly popular with friends and family.

After fourteen years, it is still exciting and interesting to me to master an Indian dish, and exciting and challenging to create a new dish and try it out with our friends. My husband has always been endlessly grateful for my cooking and never ceases to praise me. However, the true barometer of my curries has always been my brother in-law, who in the early days would often tease me about my 'mean curry'. Much time and several cook-offs (between us we have four daughters who were always the judges) have passed since then. He suggested I write this cookbook. And so, because I have also been asked by many people for recipes, here it is!

I am certainly not a chef – nor would ever claim to be – although I have always loved cooking and am happy to try my hand at almost anything. Embarking on an Indian culinary journey was interesting as I have always been addicted to spicy food, often chopping up chillies to sprinkle over western food. The new tastes were very attractive to me.

Several friends laugh at me when, after a few glasses of vino, I accidentally put the chicken in the meat sauce and the meat in the chicken sauce (they actually mimic my reaction of horror). But it all comes out fine in the end. It is not slap-happy but rather it's about understanding what makes a good base and what combines to make an appetising dish. A chicken tikka and lamb balti can end up the other way around – no problem! Similarly, it is fine to substitute spices if you don't have the necessary ingredients to hand.

I am not a cook who slaves in the kitchen all day before a dinner party or a gathering of twenty. It is known that in our house we eat rather late because, as a general rule, I never start cooking before 6pm. Often the evening's focus is over the hob, but that is because people are genuinely interested in how easy it is to cook a few curries. Curries often make for more of a supper than a dinner and are traditionally served in Britain to finish the night, not start it. Unlike other cuisines, I have never prepared and served Indian cooking as a long drawn-out dinner party. **My style is to end the evening with a feast.**

This cookbook is designed to demonstrate how simple it can be to cook a delicious Indian meal for two, ten or twenty people in a very short space of time, without complicated instructions and on a very good budget. There are tips along the way that will help..

These recipes will not teach you to cook intricate Indian cuisine, and will in no way compete with experts on such fine dining. But that is the point! The book aspires to teach those interested how to make a quick and tasty curry (and extras) with enough for everyone and on a relatively small budget, as well as how to de-mystify the process for those who long to cook the exotic foods of India.

You will notice that several of the recipes have the same base. Most of them start with oil, onions, garlic and ginger and then a mixture of different spices. It is deliberately written this way to help you become familiar with the base of each and every curry dish. You are then able to make several dishes at the same time without difficulty.

Indian cooking can be easy and even some mistakes along the way can be rectified. **Don't be afraid to experiment** and don't be too worried about getting it right. It is about confidence, not arrogance, and it is essential you enjoy it!

Before You Begin...

Which ingredients to buy

The most basic ingredients for a multitude of curries are: onions, garlic, root ginger (or ground ginger), curry powder, garam masala, turmeric, tandoori powder and tinned tomatoes and fresh coriander.

For curries with more complex flavours: peppercorns, cumin seeds, ground cumin, cloves, mustard seeds, ground coriander and coriander seeds.

Where to buy ingredients

All the ingredients in this book are available at your local supermarket. Often they can be purchased at your local convenience store, as they are becoming increasingly popular in British cooking. This book is deliberately designed to keep recipes simple and accessible by using the most basic of ingredients. With Indian cooking, people often don't know what the spices are or how to find them. The solution is to stick with a few essential ingredients that can be used for many and varied recipes.

Nevertheless, it is worthwhile hunting out your nearest Indian food suppliers. Indian communities usually have several stores located close together that can provide you with rich and diverse foods and spices at very reasonable prices. Here you can buy your spices and rice in bulk, which will save you a lot of money, as well as appropriate storage containers for them. You will also find exotic fruit, vegetables and herbs that usually you cannot find elsewhere. Along with the vegetable and fruit stalls, there is often a butcher's and a fish-monger's. A trip is well worthwhile as it provides competitively priced one-stop shopping.

Utensils

The few essential utensils are:
  – Large bowls
  – Large pots. I prefer to use a large Teflon pan (like a small wok) to cook in but a pot will suffice. Be careful not to use thin-bottomed pots as these require constant stirring of your curries to prevent burning and will not slow-cook them. A heavier-based pan is much easier to use and ensures your mixtures will not stick to the bottom when slow-cooking.
  – Wooden spoons
  – A bunch of teaspoons, tablespoons
  – A measuring jug
  – A kettle of boiling water is always good to have on hand
  – Serving dishes, platters and spoons so curries can be served hot and quickly

When marinades are required, it is always handy to have disposable gloves available not just for hygiene purposes but to protect your skin. Spices can stain the skin and chilli can burn.

Tips on Indian cooking

Oil – I always advise using olive oil as it is healthier and makes a better curry. Before starting to cook, always heat the pan first so it is hot before the oil is added. Also, be sure that the oil is hot (but not smoking) before adding the onions. This will ensure the onions absorb the oil. If the oil is not hot when the onions are added, the curry will have an oily sauce when serving.

Water – Always have a kettle of boiling hot water to hand. You may need this throughout the cooking process, particularly when cooking the spices and when each curry has been cooking for over 40 minutes. Adding approximately ½ cup of water when a curry gets dry can prevent it from burning.

Cooking Spices – It is always best to singe the spices with the onions, garlic and ginger, letting the mixture dry for a few minutes to combine and release flavours before adding any further ingredients.

Chillies – The chillies in the following recipes are Thai green or red finger chillies. I use these chillies because they are tasty and usually available throughout the year. Bullet chillies are also nice and make a good side dish when cooked. When cooking curries, chillies do add a lot of flavour but don't necessarily make the curry spicy hot. But when the chillies break or are chopped, then the heat seeps into the curry.

Hotness of Curries – As a rule I do not tend to make 'hot' curries and this is because there are usually some children along with adults dining in my home who cannot eat spicy food. Unless specified in the following recipes, each dish is made to serve people with varied tastes and requirements. What I do serve is spicy sauces alongside the dishes and I always have a plate of raw chillies and raw onions on a side dish, which people can eat with their curries. Although it sounds rather strange, raw onions (white and red) provide a nice accompaniment to spicy food.

Yoghurt – Where yoghurt is mentioned throughout the book it refers to natural yoghurt. Yoghurt can provide for many different sauces and is always handy to have around when someone shows off and eats a whole chilli. (Sugar can always help in this emergency, too.)

Meat – All the recipes in this book containing meat can be substituted with other types of meat, and it is always fun to play around with different sauces, too. Also, the longer the meat cooks, the more the flavours infuse and combine, but remember to keep stirring at regular intervals and add ¼ cup of water if the sauce is becoming too dry.

Desserts – Often when people have eaten Indian food there is not much room left for dessert. Indian food can be quite heavy and it is often better to end the dinner with something fruity, as it is light and sweet. Because of this, almost all of the desserts listed in this book have a fruit base or element to them.

STARTERS

Spicy Butternut Squash Soup

Ingredients

4	tablespoons olive oil
1	onion, finely chopped
1	garlic clove (or 2 heaped teaspoons minced garlic)
4	cups boiling water
1	butternut squash, cubed
1	teaspoon chilli powder or chilli flakes
1	teaspoon curry powder
1	teaspoon black peppercorns
½	teaspoon salt
2	cups chicken stock (or 2 tablespoons chicken stock granules dissolved in 2 cups boiling water)
½	cup cream
¼	cup chopped parsley

Heat the oil in a pan until hot, add the onions and garlic and cook for 3 minutes. Add the butternut squash, boiling water and all other ingredients. Bring to the boil and simmer for 30 minutes or until the squash is soft. Blend in a food processor and serve garnished with a spoonful of cream sprinkled with coarsely ground black pepper and chopped parsley.

Other suggestions
- Replace the chicken stock with vegetable stock if preferred.
- Replace ¼ of the butternut squash with potatoes if you desire less of a rich taste.
- This is rich and very filling and small portions are advised.

Serving: 4-6   Time: 45 minutes

Chilli Tomato Soup

Ingredients

4	tablespoons olive oil
1	onion, finely chopped
1	garlic cloves
	(or 2 heaped teaspoons minced garlic)
6	cups boiling water
10	large tomatoes, peeled
2	teaspoons chilli powder or chilli flakes
2	cups chicken stock
	(or 2 tablespoons chicken stock granules)
¼	cup chopped basil
¼	cup chopped parsley
½	cup cream
¼	cup chopped parsley
	Salt and pepper to taste

Heat the oil in a pan then add the onions and garlic and cook for 3 minutes. Add the boiling water, tomatoes and all other ingredients. Bring to the boil and simmer for 30 minutes or until the tomatoes are soft. Blend together in a food processor and serve with basil garnish.

Other suggestions
* Replace the chicken stock with vegetable stock if preferred.

Serving: 4-6   Time: 35 minutes

Chicken Wings Indian Style

Ingredients

4	tablespoons olive oil
2	heaped teaspoons minced garlic
1	teaspoon ginger shavings (or 1 teaspoon ground ginger)
2	teaspoons chilli powder
3	tablespoons tandoori paste
2	tablespoons tomato puree
1½	tablespoons natural yoghurt
12-16	chicken wings
	Salt and pepper

Mix all the spices, tomato puree, yoghurt and oil until fully combined, then add chicken and smother with sauce. (Wearing a plastic glove is helpful.) Bake in the oven on a tray for 45 minutes.

Other suggestions
- The chicken is nicer if marinated for 12-24 hours.
- You can substitute the chicken wings with lamb, chicken or beef chunks, or butterfly prawns.

Serving: 4-6   Time: 1 hour

Grilled Tikka Chops

Ingredients
4	tablespoons olive oil
1	garlic clove (or 2 heaped teaspoons minced garlic)
1	teaspoon ginger shavings (or 1 teaspoon ground ginger)
1	teaspoon chilli powder
1	tablespoon garam masala
2	tablespoons tandoori powder
2	tablespoons finely chopped fresh coriander
1	tablespoon tomato puree
2	tablespoons natural yoghurt
8	chops Sprinkle of salt and pepper

Optional
1	teaspoon mint sauce

Mix all the spices, tomato puree, yoghurt and oil until fully combined, then add meat and smother with sauce. (Wearing a plastic glove is helpful.) Place under a medium-high heated grill until fully cooked and crisp, turning when needed.

"Natural yogurt works a treat in marinades!"

Other suggestions
- The meat is nicer if marinated for 12-24 hours.
- Serve with yoghurt and mint sauce.
- Serve with a small salad and garnishing of mint and coriander leaves.
- Add chillies if you want it spicier.
- You can substitute the chops with lamb, chicken or beef chunks, or butterfly prawns.

Serving: 4-6   Time: 40-50 minutes

Lamb Kidneys

Ingredients

4	tablespoons olive oil
1	onion, finely chopped
2	cloves
2	green finger chillies
2	garlic cloves
	(or 2 heaped teaspoons minced garlic)
1	teaspoon ginger shavings
	(or 1 teaspoon ground ginger)
1	teaspoon curry powder
1	tablespoon garam masala
1	tablespoon tandoori powder
1	teaspoon mustard seeds
500	grams lamb kidneys
3	heaped tablespoons tomato puree
1	cup boiling water
	Salt to taste

Heat the oil in a pan until hot then add the onions, cloves and chillies and cook on medium heat for 2-3 minutes until transparent. Add the garlic and ginger and cook for 3 minutes. Add the spices (curry powder, garam masala, tandoori powder and mustard seeds) and cook dry until singed. Add the kidneys, cover them with spices and cook for a further 5 minutes. Add the water and tomato puree, bring to the boil then reduce heat and cook for 25 minutes. If the curry starts sticking to the bottom of the pan, add half a cup of water but try to keep the mixture dry and not too watery. Add salt to taste a few minutes before serving.

Serving: 6-8   Time: 45 minutes

Grilled Tikka Chicken Drumsticks

Ingredients

4	tablespoons olive oil
2	heaped teaspoons minced garlic
1	teaspoon ginger shavings (or 1 teaspoon ground ginger)
1	teaspoon chilli powder
2	tablespoons tandoori powder
2	tablespoons finely chopped fresh coriander
2	tablespoons tomato puree
1½	tablespoons natural yoghurt
8	chicken drumsticks
	Salt and pepper

Optional

1	teaspoon chopped fresh coriander

Mix all the spices, tomato puree, yoghurt and oil until fully combined, then add chicken and smother with sauce. (Wearing a plastic glove is helpful.) Place under a medium-high heated grill until fully cooked and crisp, turning when needed.

Other suggestions

- The chicken is nicer if marinated for 12-24 hours.
- Before serving, wrap tinfoil around the base of each drumstick so it is easier to hold.
- You can substitute the chicken with chops, lamb or beef chunks, or butterfly prawns.

"Kids love 'em too!"

Serving: 4-6   Time: 40-50 minutes

Hot and Spicy Kebabs

Ingredients

500 ml Vegetable oil for shallow frying
4 tablespoons olive oil
1 teaspoon ground white pepper
1 teaspoon chilli powder
2 green finger chillies, chopped
2 onions, finely chopped
2 garlic cloves
  (or 2 heaped teaspoons minced garlic)
1 teaspoon ginger shavings
  (or 1 teaspoon ground ginger)
1 tablespoon curry powder
1 tablespoon garam masala
1 teaspoon mustard seeds
1 teaspoon ground coriander
2 heaped tablespoons tomato puree
500 grams beef sausage meat
1 egg
½ cup breadcrumbs
1 tablespoon flour
  Salt to taste
  Pan of light vegetable oil for shallow frying

Mix all ingredients (except flour) together in a large bowl until completely combined. Roll into balls or oblong shapes. Coat the kebabs in flour and shallow fry (on high) in batches for 10 minutes. Be sure that the oil covers the kebabs. Drain on tissue or kitchen towel before serving.

Serve hot or cold with chutneys and raita.

Serving: 6-8   Time: 40 minutes

Simple Baked Tomatoes with Almonds

Ingredients

10	large tomatoes, halved
4	tablespoons olive oil
1	garlic clove
	(or 2 heaped teaspoons minced garlic)
1	teaspoon cumin seeds
1	teaspoon ground coriander
1	teaspoon chilli powder or chilli flakes
1	cup vegetable stock
100	grams almond flakes
	Salt and pepper to taste

Heat the oil in a pan then add all the ingredients. Cook for 10 minutes and simmer into a paste. Spread over the top of the tomato halves. Place the tomato halves on an oven tray and cook for 25 minutes on 190 C (Gas Mark 5).

Other suggestions
- Add chopped mushrooms if preferred.

Serving: 4-6   Time: 35 minutes

Stuffed Chillies

Ingredients
10   large red bullet chillies, split down the middle and seeded

Stuffing
4   tablespoons olive oil
1   onion, finely chopped
1   teaspoon minced garlic
½   teaspoon mustard seeds
½   teaspoon cumin seeds
½   teaspoon chilli flakes
½   cup chopped fresh coriander
2   cups mashed potatoes
¼   cup grated paneer cheese
¼   cup grated mozzarella cheese
     Salt and pepper to taste

Heat the oil in a pan until hot then add the split bullet chillies. Cook on a low heat for 3 minutes until the chillies are soft but not completely cooked. Remove from pan and set aside.

Heat the oil in the pan again and when hot, add onion and cook for 3 minutes. Add garlic, cumin seeds and mustard seeds and cook for 5 minutes. In a separate bowl, add the onion mix to the remaining ingredients and combine until all the spices are blended with the potatoes and cheeses. Add salt and pepper to taste.

Stuff chillies with mixture, lay them on a rack and cook in the oven for 20 minutes at 190 C (Gas Mark 5).

Serving: 4-6   Time: 45 minutes

Masala Chops

Ingredients

4	tablespoons olive oil
4	onions, sliced
2	garlic cloves
	(or 4 heaped teaspoons minced garlic)
1	teaspoon chilli powder
½	teaspoon mustard powder
2	tablespoons garam masala
1	teaspoon turmeric
3	tomatoes, chopped,
	(or ½ tin chopped tomatoes)
1	tablespoon natural yoghurt
8	chops
	Salt and pepper
1	cup boiling water

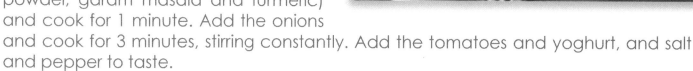

Heat the oil in a pan until hot, add the garlic and all the spices (chilli, mustard powder, garam masala and turmeric) and cook for 1 minute. Add the onions and cook for 3 minutes, stirring constantly. Add the tomatoes and yoghurt, and salt and pepper to taste.

Wrap the ends of the chops in tinfoil and grill on high for 5 minutes on both sides.

Place chops in roasting dish and cover with masala sauce, water and onions and cook for 45 minutes at 190 C (Gas Mark 5).

Other suggestions
- Serve with raita.
- Add chillies garlic if you want it spicier.
- You can substitute the chops with lamb, chicken or beef chunks, or butterfly prawns.

Serving: 4   Time: 1 hour

Prawn Puri

Ingredients

4	tablespoons olive oil
1	onion, finely chopped
2	garlic cloves (or 2 heaped teaspoons minced garlic)
1	teaspoon ginger shavings (or 1 teaspoon ground ginger)
1	teaspoon curry powder
2	heaped tablespoons turmeric
500	grams fresh or thawed prawns
½	tin chopped tomatoes
½	tin coconut cream
	Salt

Heat the oil in a pan until hot, add the onions and cook on medium heat for 2-3 minutes until transparent. Add the garlic and ginger and cook for 3 minutes. Add the spices (curry powder and turmeric) and cook for 2 minutes. Add the prawns, tomatoes and coconut cream and cook for 5 minutes. Add water to just cover the prawns. Bring to the boil, reduce the heat and cook for 10 minutes. Add salt to taste.

Serve on chapati bread.

Serving: 4-6   Time: 20 minutes

Pakora

Ingredients

Vegetable oil for shallow frying

½	cup water
1	cup chickpea flour
½	teaspoon ground coriander
½	teaspoon ground cumin
½	teaspoon turmeric
½	teaspoon garam masala
½	teaspoon chilli powder
1	teaspoon crushed garlic
½	teaspoon salt
1	cup cooked potato, cut into large slices
1	cup cooked cauliflower, cut into florets
1	cup cooked whole, seeded chillies
1	cup onion rings

Sift the flour in a large bowl and add the coriander, cumin, turmeric, garam masala, garlic and salt. Slowly add water and mix thoroughly to form a batter. Beat mixture to make it lighter.

Heat the oil on high in a large pan. Once hot, reduce heat to 190 C (gas mark 5). Coat the potato, cauliflower, chillies and onion rings in the batter and shallow fry in the oil for 3-4 minutes. Once cooked, drain on kitchen towel.

Serve hot or cold with chutneys and raita.

Serving: 6-8   Time: 40 minutes

VEGETARIAN

Dried Lentil Soup (Tarka Dal)

Ingredients

4	tablespoons olive oil
2	onions, finely chopped
1	teaspoon peppercorns (or coarsely ground black pepper)
2	garlic cloves (or 2 heaped teaspoons minced garlic)
½	teaspoon ginger shavings (or 1 teaspoon ground ginger)
3	red finger chillies
1	teaspoon curry powder
2	tablespoons turmeric
1	teaspoon garam masala
1½	cups lentils
2	tablespoons finely chopped fresh coriander
3	tomatoes, freshly chopped
	Salt

Optional

You can replace the lentils with any other type of dal (i.e. dried bean pulses or split peas), or experiment with a combination of different ones.

Wash lentils thoroughly in a sieve until water runs clear. Cover with 6 cups of water and bring to the boil. Reduce heat and simmer for 2 hours. (Alternatively, cook in a pressure cooker for 10-15 minutes). Add water if needed.

In a separate pan heat the oil. When hot, add the onions and cook until transparent. Add the garlic and ginger and cook for 3 minutes. Add the chillies and spices and cook for 5 minutes until slightly singed. Add a sprinkle of water as needed. Add the tomatoes and half of the chopped coriander and cook for 20 minutes. Combine cooked lentils and water with sauce mixture and whisk until smooth. Add salt and cook on a low heat for 5 minutes. Before serving, sprinkle with coriander. Serve with chapati or rice or as an accompaniment to the main dish.

Serving: 4-6   Time: 40 minutes, but needs an extra 2 hours if you don't use a pressure cooker.

Potato and Egg Curry (Aloo)

Ingredients

4	tablespoons olive oil
2	onions, finely chopped
1	teaspoon peppercorns (or coarsely ground black pepper)
1	garlic clove (or 2 heaped teaspoons minced garlic)
1	teaspoon ginger shavings (or 1 teaspoon ground ginger)
1	heaped tablespoon curry powder
1	heaped tablespoon turmeric
½	kilo cooked new potatoes
6	hard boiled eggs, halved
	Salt

Optional

½   teaspoon cumin seeds

Heat the oil in a pan until hot, add the onions and cook on medium heat for 2-3 minutes until transparent. Add the garlic, ginger and optional ingredients and cook for 3 minutes. Add spices (curry powder and turmeric) and cook dry until singed. Add potatoes and eggs and cook for 10 minutes or until the egg yolk has combined with sauce, stirring every couple of minutes. Add salt to taste.

Serve with rice or chapati bread and a side salad.

Other suggestions

- Garnish with chives or chopped spring onions before serving.

"My favourite!"

Serving: 4-6   Time: 40 minutes

Spinach with Paneer Cheese (Sag Paneer)

Ingredients

4	tablespoons olive oil
1	onion, finely chopped
½	teaspoon peppercorns (or coarsely ground black pepper)
1	teaspoon chilli powder
2	garlic cloves (or 2 heaped teaspoons minced garlic)
1	teaspoon ginger shavings (or 1 teaspoon ground ginger)
1	heaped tablespoon curry powder
½	teaspoon turmeric
1	heaped tablespoon garam masala
½	tin chopped tomatoes
2	heaped tablespoons tomato puree
½	kilo frozen spinach (or 2 tins leaf spinach)
30	grams paneer cheese
	Salt

Optional

2	cloves
½	teaspoon cumin seeds

Heat the oil in a pan until hot, add the onions and cook on medium heat for 2-3 minutes until transparent. Add the garlic, ginger and optional ingredients and cook for 3 minutes. Add the spices (chilli, pepper, curry powder, turmeric and garam masala) and cook dry until singed. Add the tomatoes and spinach and cook for 5 minutes. Add the paneer and tomato puree and cook for 10 minutes. Add salt to taste.

Serve with rice or chapati bread and side salad.

Other suggestions

- You can leave out the paneer if preferred.

Serving: 4-6   Time: 30 minutes

Mixed Vegetable Curry

Ingredients

4	tablespoons olive oil
3	onions, cut into quarters
1	teaspoon whole black peppercorns
1	teaspoon chilli powder
2	garlic cloves (or 2 heaped teaspoons minced garlic)
1	teaspoon ginger shavings (or 1 teaspoon ground ginger)
1	heaped tablespoon curry powder
1	heaped tablespoon turmeric
1	heaped teaspoon garam masala
1	teaspoon ground cumin powder
4	fresh tomatoes, cut into quarters
¼	cauliflower
10	new potatoes
1	green pepper
1	red pepper
4	cups water
	Salt

Heat the oil in a pan until hot, add the onions and tomatoes and cook for 2-3 minutes. Add the peppercorns, garlic, ginger, chilli and other spices (curry powder, turmeric, garam masala and cumin) and cook for 5 minutes. Add the vegetables and water, bring to the boil and cook for 20 minutes or until the potatoes are fully cooked and the water has reduced. Add salt to taste.

Serve on a bed of rice, with a side salad.

Other suggestions
- You can replace any of the vegetables with other preferred and/or available vegetables.
- You can also pre-cook the vegetables and use the stock instead of water if you want the dish to be ready more quickly.

Serving: 4-6   Time: 40 minutes

Chickpea and Sweet Corn Curry

Ingredients

4	tablespoons olive oil
2	onions, finely chopped
1	tablespoon peppercorns
1	teaspoon chilli powder
2	garlic cloves
	(or 2 heaped teaspoons minced garlic)
1	clove
1	teaspoon ginger shavings
	(or 1 teaspoon ground ginger)
1	teaspoon curry powder
1	heaped tablespoon turmeric
1	teaspoon garam masala
5	fresh tomatoes, chopped
500	grams cooked chickpeas
	(or 500 grams drained weight of
	tinned chickpeas)
150-200 grams sweet corn	
	Salt

Heat the oil in a pan until hot, add the onions and cook on medium heat for 2-3 minutes until transparent. Add peppercorns, chilli, garlic, clove, ginger and cook for 3 minutes. Add curry powder, turmeric and garam masala and cook dry until singed. Add the chickpeas, sweet corn and tomatoes and cook for 15 minutes, adding water if getting too dry or if you prefer it saucier. Add salt to taste.

Serve on a bed of rice.

Serving: 4-6   Time: 30 minutes

Cauliflower Chilli

Ingredients

4	tablespoons olive oil
1	onion, finely chopped
1	teaspoon finely ground white pepper
2	teaspoons chilli powder
2	garlic cloves
	(or 2 heaped teaspoons minced garlic)
1	teaspoon ginger shavings
	(or 1 teaspoon ground ginger)
1	heaped tablespoon curry powder
1	heaped tablespoon turmeric
1	teaspoon cumin seeds
1	teaspoon coriander paste
	(or 1 tablespoon finely chopped coriander)
½	tin chopped tomatoes
1	tablespoon tomato puree
1	large cauliflower
4	cups water
	Salt

Heat the oil in a pan until hot, add the onions and cook on medium heat for 2-3 minutes until transparent. Add the garlic and ginger and cook for 2 minutes. Add the spices (pepper, chilli, curry powder, turmeric and cumin) and cook dry until singed. Add the tomatoes, water and cauliflower and cook for 15 minutes. Add the coriander and tomato puree and cook for 5 minutes or until water has reduced. Add salt to taste.

Serve on a bed of rice, with a side salad.

Serving: 4-6   Time: 30 minutes

Potato Cakes Smothered in Chickpea Curry and Yoghurt

Ingredients

Potato cakes

4	tablespoons vegetable oil
1	teaspoon ground coriander
1	teaspoon cumin powder
1	teaspoon chilli powder
6	cups mashed potatoes
1	egg
	Salt and pepper to taste

Chickpea curry

4	tablespoons olive oil
2	tins cooked chickpeas, drained
2	onions, finely chopped
1	garlic clove
2	tablespoons turmeric
1	teaspoon garam masala
½	tin chopped tomatoes
1	cup yoghurt
½	cup chopped fresh coriander
	Salt and pepper to taste

Potato cakes

Mix the mashed potatoes with all the other ingredients except the oil. Roll into 6 large balls. In a pan, heat the oil until hot then lay the balls in the pan, flattening with an egg slice. Reduce the heat to medium and cook the potato cakes for 5 minutes on each side or until golden. Set aside and drain on a tissue or kitchen towel.

Chickpea curry

Heat the oil in a pan until hot, add the onion and cook for 3 minutes. Add the garlic and spices (garam masala and turmeric) and cook for 3 minutes. Add the chickpeas and chopped tomatoes and cook for 15 minutes. Add salt and pepper.

Lay the potato cakes on the base of a plate or large dish. Pour the curry over the centre of the arranged potato cakes. Garnish the middle of the curry with the yoghurt and coriander.

Other suggestions
- You can substitute the chickpeas with other vegetables if preferred.

Serving: 4-6   Time: 50 minutes

Spinach with Potatoes (Sag Aloo)

Ingredients

4	tablespoons olive oil
1	onion, finely chopped
½	teaspoon peppercorns (or coarsely ground black pepper)
1	teaspoon chilli powder
2	garlic cloves (or 2 heaped teaspoons minced garlic)
1	teaspoon ginger shavings (or 1 teaspoon ground ginger)
1	teaspoon curry powder
½	teaspoon tandoori powder
1	heaped tablespoon garam masala
1	teaspoon turmeric
½	teaspoon cumin seeds
1	tin chopped tomatoes
2	heaped tablespoons tomato puree
500 grams frozen spinach (or 2 tins leaf spinach)	
500 grams of cooked new potatoes	
Salt	

Heat the oil in a pan until hot, add the onions and cook on medium heat for 2-3 minutes until transparent. Add garlic, ginger and cook for 3 minutes. Add spices (chilli, pepper, curry powder, turmeric, garam masala, cumin seeds and tandoori powder) and cook dry until singed. Add the tinned tomatoes and the spinach and cook for 5 minutes. Add the potatoes and tomato puree and cook for 10 minutes. Add salt to taste.

Serve with rice or chapati bread and a side salad.

"Don't be afraid to add chilli at the start if you want it hotter!"

Serving: 4-6   Time: 30 minutes

Fried Aubergines

Ingredients

4	tablespoons olive oil
1	onion, finely chopped
½	teaspoon peppercorns (or coarsely ground black pepper)
1	teaspoon chilli powder
2	garlic cloves (or 2 heaped teaspoons minced garlic)
1	teaspoon ginger shavings (or 1 teaspoon ground ginger)
1	heaped tablespoon garam masala
1	teaspoon turmeric
2	tomatoes, freshly chopped
1	cup boiling water
2	heaped tablespoons tomato puree
4	small aubergines, sliced
¼	cup chopped fresh coriander
	Salt

Heat the oil in a pan until hot, add the onions and cook on medium heat for 2-3 minutes until transparent. Add the garlic and ginger and cook for 3 minutes. Add the spices (chilli, pepper, turmeric and garam masala) and cook dry until singed. Add the water, tomatoes and tomato puree and cook on medium heat for 5 minutes. Add the sliced aubergines and cook on medium heat for 25 minutes. Add salt to taste and toss in coriander just before serving.

Serve with rice or chapati bread and side salad.

Serving: 4   Time: 30 minutes

Smothered Mushrooms

"This is a lovely dish that can also work well as a starter"

Ingredients

4	tablespoons olive oil
2	tablespoons butter
1	onion, finely chopped
1	teaspoon ground white pepper
1	teaspoon chilli powder
1	teaspoon dried chilli flakes
3	garlic cloves (or 3 heaped teaspoons minced garlic)
1	teaspoon ginger shavings (or 1 teaspoon ground ginger)
2	chopped red peppers
2	chopped celery sticks
1	cup vegetable stock
4	fresh tomatoes, cut into quarters
8	portabella mushrooms (stalks removed)
1	cup chopped fresh coriander
	Salt

Mixture

Heat the oil in a pan then add the onions, 2 garlic cloves and the ginger shavings and cook for 3 minutes. Add the pepper, chilli powder, peppers, celery, tomatoes and vegetable stock and bring to the boil. Simmer for 20 minutes or until the water has reduced.

Mushrooms

Heat butter in a pan, adding the chilli flakes and remaining garlic when melted. Add the mushrooms and cook for 5 minutes each side. Place mushrooms in oven dish and smother with mixture. Bake in the oven for 10 minutes on 220 C (Gas Mark 6).

Sprinkle with coriander and serve with any other curry.

Other suggestions
- You can add a mango while cooking if you prefer a more fruity taste.
- This dish is also a good starter.

Serving: 4-6   Time: 40 minutes

Vegetarian Pilau

Ingredients

4	tablespoons olive oil
1	onion, finely chopped
1	clove
2	whole chillies
2	garlic cloves
	(or 2 heaped teaspoons minced garlic)
1	teaspoon ginger shavings
	(or 1 teaspoon ground ginger)
1	teaspoon black pepper
1	teaspoon curry powder
½	teaspoon garam masala
½	teaspoon turmeric
500	grams mixed vegetables
1	red onion, quartered
3	tomatoes, freshly chopped
3	cups basmati rice, washed
3	cups boiling water
1	teaspoon butter
	Salt to taste

Heat the oil in a pan until hot then add the onion and cook for 2 minutes. Add the clove and the whole chillies and cook for 1 minute being careful not to break the chillies. Add the garlic, ginger and other spices (pepper, curry powder, garam masala and turmeric), the mixed vegetables, red onion and tomatoes and cook for 5 minutes. Mix in the rice, water, butter and salt and bring to the boil, cover and reduce heat to low and cook for 20 minutes.

Serve with sprinkled coriander.

Serving: 4-6   Time: 35 minutes

CHICKEN DISHES

Butter Chicken

Ingredients

4	tablespoons olive oil
1	onion, finely chopped
3	heaped tablespoons butter
1	teaspoon peppercorns (or coarsely ground black pepper)
2	garlic cloves (or 2 heaped teaspoons minced garlic)
1	teaspoon ginger shavings (or 1 teaspoon ground ginger)
2	tablespoons ground almonds
1	teaspoon cumin seeds
1	teaspoon ground cinnamon
1	heaped tablespoon turmeric
1	teaspoon garam masala
1	tablespoon tomato puree
½	cup cream
4	chicken breasts, cubed
	Salt

"Sprinkling with coriander or spring onions always tastes and looks nicer"

You can replace chicken breasts with chicken pieces (thighs are great – tastier and cheaper but continue cooking until chicken falls off the bone). Add the garlic and ginger and cook for 3 minutes. Add the spices (almond, cumin seeds, cinnamon, turmeric and garam masala) and cook dry until singed. Add the chicken breasts, let spices cover them and cook for 5 minutes. Add tomato puree and water to just cover the chicken, bring to the boil, reduce heat and cook for 30 minutes. If the curry starts sticking to the bottom of the pan, add a little water. Add salt to taste a few minutes before serving along with ½ cup cream.

Serve with rice or chapati bread and a side salad.

Other suggestions
- Sprinkle with freshly chopped coriander or chopped spring onions before serving.
- Add chillies with garlic if you want it spicier.

Serving: 4-6   Time: 50 minutes

Easy Chicken Curry (Chicken Sak)

Ingredients

4	tablespoons olive oil
3	onions, finely chopped
1	teaspoon peppercorns (or coarsely ground black pepper)
2	garlic cloves (or 2 heaped teaspoons minced garlic)
1	teaspoon ginger shavings (or 1 teaspoon ground ginger)
2	heaped tablespoons turmeric
1	heaped tablespoon garam masala
1	tin chopped tomatoes (or 3 tomatoes, freshly chopped)
4	chicken breasts, cubed
	Salt

Optional

2	cloves
½	teaspoon cumin seeds

Heat the oil in a pan until hot, add the onions and cook on medium heat for 2-3 minutes until transparent. Add the garlic, ginger and optional ingredients and cook for 3 minutes. Add the spices (turmeric and garam masala) and cook dry until singed. Add the chicken breasts, cover them with spices and cook for 5 minutes. Add the tomatoes, bring to the boil then reduce heat and cook for 30 minutes. If the curry starts sticking to the bottom of the pan, add a half a cup of water. Add salt to taste a few minutes before serving.

Serve with rice or chapati bread and a side salad.

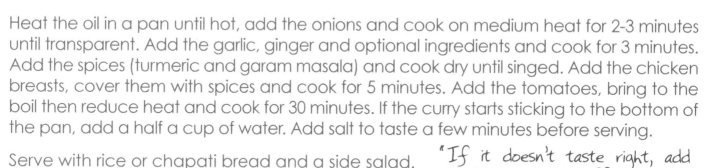

"If it doesn't taste right, add a little more salt. If too salty, throw in a few peeled potatoes to soak it up and remove before serving"

Other suggestions

- Sprinkle with freshly chopped coriander before serving.
- Add cooked potatoes.
- Add chillies with garlic if you want it spicier.
- You can replace chicken breasts with chicken pieces (thighs are great – tastier and cheaper, but do remove the skin but continue cooking until chicken falls off the bone).

Serving: 4-6   Time: 50 minutes

Chicken Tikka Masala

Ingredients

4	tablespoons olive oil
2	onions, finely chopped
1	teaspoon coriander seeds or ground coriander
1	heaped teaspoon chilli powder (or 3 whole green finger chillies)
2	garlic cloves (or 2 heaped teaspoons minced garlic)
1	teaspoon ginger shavings (or 1 teaspoon ground ginger)
½	teaspoon nutmeg
1	heaped tablespoon garam masala
2	heaped tablespoons tandoori powder
4	chicken breasts, cubed
4	tablespoons tomato puree
	Water
	Salt

Heat the oil in a pan until hot, add the onions and cook on medium heat for 2-3 minutes until transparent. Add the garlic and ginger and cook for 3 minutes. Add the spices (coriander seeds, nutmeg, garam masala, tandoori powder and chilli powder) and cook dry until singed. Add the chicken breasts, cover them in the spices and cook for 5 minutes.

"Colour is always a good indication of how it will taste and how it should look"

Add the tomato puree and then water to just cover the chicken. Bring to the boil, reduce heat and cook for 30 minutes. Add salt to taste.

Serve with rice or chapati bread and side salad.

Other suggestions

- Add 1 tablespoon of sugar or honey if you prefer the dish sweeter.
- Add ½ cup cream to make it creamier, or ½ cup of yoghurt to lessen the richness.
- You can replace chicken breasts with chicken pieces (thighs are great – tastier and cheaper but continue cooking until chicken falls off the bone).

Serving: 4-6   Time: 40 minutes

Coconut Chicken

Ingredients

- 4 tablespoons olive oil
- 2 onions, finely chopped
- 1 teaspoon peppercorns
  (or coarsely ground black pepper)
- 2 garlic cloves
  (or 2 heaped teaspoons minced garlic)
- 1 teaspoon ginger shavings
  (or 1 teaspoon ground ginger)
- 1 heaped tablespoon curry powder
- 1 heaped tablespoon turmeric
- 4 chicken breasts, cubed
- 250 ml coconut milk
  Salt

Heat the oil in a pan until hot, add the onions and cook on medium heat for 2-3 minutes until transparent. Add the garlic and ginger and cook for 3 minutes. Add the spices (pepper, curry powder and turmeric) and cook dry until singed. Add the chicken breasts, cover them in the spices and cook for 5 minutes. Add the coconut milk then add water to just cover the chicken. Bring to the boil, then reduce the heat and cook for 30 minutes. Add salt to taste.

Serve with rice or chapati bread and side salad.

Other suggestions

- Add cooked potatoes.
- You can replace chicken breasts with chicken pieces (thighs are great – tastier and cheaper but continue cooking until chicken falls off the bone).

Serving: 4-6   Time: 45 minutes

Chicken on Fire

Ingredients

4	tablespoons olive oil
1	tablespoon butter
1	onion, finely chopped
2	teaspoons peppercorns (or coarsely ground black pepper)
2	cloves
2	garlic cloves (or 2 heaped teaspoons minced garlic)
1	teaspoon ginger shavings (or 1 teaspoon ground ginger)
1	tablespoon chilli powder
1	teaspoon cumin seeds
1	teaspoon mustard seeds
1	heaped tablespoons curry powder
1	teaspoon garam masala
1	heaped tablespoon tandoori powder
1	tablespoon lime juice
2	heaped tablespoons tomato puree
2	cups water
4	chicken breasts, cubed
	Salt

Heat the oil in a pan until hot, add the onions and cook on medium heat for 2-3 minutes until transparent. Add the garlic and ginger and cook for 3 minutes. Add the spices (pepper, cloves, chilli powder, cumin seeds, mustard seeds, curry powder, garam masala and tandoori powder) and cook dry until singed. Add the chicken breasts, cover them in the spices and cook for 5 minutes. Add water, lime juice and tomato puree and bring to the boil. Reduce heat and cook for 30 minutes. If the curry starts sticking to the bottom of the pan, add a little water. Add salt to taste a few minutes before serving.

Serve with rice or chapati bread and a side salad.

Serving: 4-6   Time: 50 minutes

Chicken Chilli

Ingredients

4	tablespoons olive oil
2	onions, finely chopped
1	teaspoon ground white pepper
1	clove
1	heaped tablespoon chilli powder
5	whole green or red finger chillies
2	garlic cloves (or 2 heaped teaspoons minced garlic)
1	heaped tablespoon curry powder
1	heaped tablespoon tandoori powder
4	chicken breasts, cubed
½	tin chopped tomatoes
1	tablespoon tomato puree
	Water
	Salt

Heat the oil in a pan until hot, add the onions and cook on medium heat for 2-3 minutes until transparent. Add the garlic and cook for 3 minutes. Add the spices (pepper, chilli powder, curry powder and tandoori powder) and cook dry until singed. Add the chillies and chicken breasts, cover them in the spices and cook for 5 minutes (be careful not to break chillis). Add the chopped tomatoes and tomato puree, then add water to just cover the chicken. Bring to the boil, then reduce heat and cook for 30 minutes. Add salt to taste.

Sprinkle with coriander. Serve with rice or chapati bread and a side salad.

Other suggestions
- Add more chillies and chilli powder if you prefer a hotter flavour.
- You can replace 1 teaspoon of chilli powder with ½ teaspoon dried chilli.
- You can replace chicken breasts with chicken pieces (thighs are great – tastier and cheaper but continue cooking until chicken falls off the bone).

Serving: 4-6   Time: 50 minutes

"If you put chillies in whole, they will not make the dish hot but will give it flavour. The more the chillies are chopped, the hotter the dish"

Chicken with Onions

Ingredients

4	tablespoons olive oil
1	tablespoon butter
2	garlic cloves
	(or 2 heaped teaspoons minced garlic)
1	teaspoon ginger shavings
	(or 1 teaspoon ground ginger)
1	teaspoon curry powder
1	heaped tablespoon turmeric
1	teaspoon ground coriander
1	teaspoon cumin seeds
1	cup yoghurt
5	onions, cut into rings
4	chicken breasts, cubed
	Salt and pepper

Heat the oil in a pan. Sear the chicken for 5 minutes then remove from the pan. In the pan, add the oil and butter and when hot add garlic, ginger, curry powder, turmeric, coriander and cumin. When singed, add chicken and cook dry (add 4 tablespoons of water if it sticks to the pan). When cooked remove from the pan.

Add onion rings to the cooking juices and cook until transparent. Remove and keep warm until serving.

Place chicken back in the pan and add salt, pepper and yoghurt and cook until the yoghurt is soaked up by chicken.

Serve with rice and a salad.

Other suggestions
• Add chillies if you want it spicier.

Serving: 4-6   Time: 55 minutes

Chicken Pilau

Ingredients

4	tablespoons olive oil
1	onion, finely chopped
1	clove
1	teaspoon cumin seeds
3	whole chillies
2	garlic cloves
	(or 2 heaped teaspoons minced garlic)
1	teaspoon ginger shavings
	(or 1 teaspoon ground ginger)
1	teaspoon ground black pepper
1	teaspoon curry powder
1	teaspoon garam masala
1	teaspoon turmeric
4	chicken breasts, cubed
2	chopped tomotoes
3	cups basmati rice, washed
3	cups boiling water
1	teaspoon butter
1	tablespoon salt
¼	cups chopped fresh coriander

Heat the oil in a pan. Sear the chicken for 5 minutes then remove from the pan. Reheat the oil in the pan and when hot add the onion and cook for 2 minutes. Then add the clove, cumin seeds and the whole chillies and cook for 1 minute being careful not to break the chillies. Mix in the garlic, ginger and spices (pepper, curry powder, garam masala and turmeric), then add the tomatoes and cook for 5 minutes. Add the chicken, basmati rice and salt and mix together, cooking on high for 2 minutes until the chicken and rice are coated in spices. Add boiling water and butter and bring to the boil. When boiling, cover and reduce heat to low and cook for 30 minutes.

Serve with sprinkled coriander.

Serving: 4-6   Time: 55 minutes

Chicken and Nut Curry

Ingredients

4	tablespoons olive oil
1	onion, finely chopped
1	teaspoon peppercorns (or coarsely ground black pepper)
2	garlic cloves (or 2 heaped teaspoons minced garlic)
1	teaspoon ginger shavings (or 1 teaspoon ground ginger)
1	teaspoon ground cinnamon
2	heaped tablespoons curry powder
1	teaspoon garam masala
1	teaspoon turmeric
½	cup yoghurt
4	chicken breasts, cubed
100	grams cashew nuts
3	cups boiling water
1	tablespoon chopped parsley
1	tablespoon chopped fresh coriander
	Salt

Heat the oil in a pan until hot, add the onions and cook on medium heat for 2-3 minutes until transparent. Add the garlic and ginger and cook for 3 minutes. Add spices (pepper, cinnamon, curry powder, garam masala and turmeric) and cook dry until singed. Add chicken breasts, let spices cover them and cook for 5 minutes. Add water, nuts and salt and bring to the boil. Reduce heat and cook for 30 minutes. Add yoghurt and cook for 5 minutes.

Serve with rice or chapati bread and a side salad garnished with parsley and coriander.

Other suggestions
- Add chillies with garlic if you want it spicier.

Serving: 4-6   Time: 50 minutes

Chicken with Cabbage and Leek

Ingredients

4   tablespoons olive oil
2   onions, finely chopped
2   garlic cloves (or 2 heaped teaspoons minced garlic)
1   teaspoon ground white pepper
1   clove
1   heaped teaspoon chilli powder
1   teaspoon ground coriander powder
1   heaped tablespoon curry powder
1   heaped tablespoons turmeric
4   chicken breasts, cubed
3   chopped tomatoes
1   cup chopped green cabbage
1   cup chopped leeks
1   cup boiling water
    Salt

Heat the oil in a pan until hot, add the onions and cook on medium heat for 2-3 minutes until transparent. Add the garlic and cook for 3 minutes. Add spices (pepper, clove, chilli powder, coriander, curry powder and turmeric) and cook dry until singed. Add chicken breasts, let spices cover them and cook for 10 minutes. Add chopped tomato and vegetables. Add water and bring to the boil. Reduce heat and cook for 15 minutes. Add salt to taste.

Sprinkle with freshly chopped fresh coriander.

Serve with rice or chapati bread and a side salad.

Serving: 4-6   Time: 45 minutes

Chicken Korma

Ingredients

4	tablespoons olive oil
2	onions, finely chopped
2	garlic cloves
	(or 2 heaped teaspoons minced garlic)
1	teaspoon ground white pepper
1	heaped tablespoon curry powder
1	heaped tablespoons garam masala
1	teaspoon ground coriander
3	tablespoons fromage frais
4	chicken breasts, cubed
2	tablespoons ground almonds
2	cups boiling water
	Salt

Heat the oil in a pan until hot, add the onions and cook on medium heat for 2-3 minutes until transparent. Add the garlic and cook for 3 minutes. Add spices (pepper, curry powder, garam masala and ground coriander) and cook dry until singed. Add chicken breasts, let spices cover them and cook for 10 minutes. Add water and bring to the boil. Reduce heat and cook for 15 minutes. Add salt to taste. Just before serving add fromage frais and serve with sprinkled almonds.

Sprinkle with freshly chopped fresh coriander.

Serve with rice or chapati bread and a side salad.

Serving: 4-6   Time: 45 minutes

MEAT DISHES

Beef and Pepper Curry

Ingredients

4 tablespoons olive oil
1 teaspoon peppercorns (or coarsely ground black pepper)
2 onions, finely chopped
2 garlic cloves (or 2 heaped teaspoons minced garlic)
1 teaspoon ginger shavings (or 1 teaspoon ground ginger)
2 cloves
 Sprinkle of mustard seeds
½ teaspoon curry powder
½ teaspoon turmeric
1 heaped tablespoon tandoori powder
1 heaped tablespoon garam masala
3 heaped tablespoons tomato puree
500 grams braising or stewing steak, cubed
2 red peppers
2 cups water
 Salt

Optional
½ teaspoon cumin seeds

"Always over spice rather than under spice"

Heat the oil in a pan until hot, add the onions and cook on medium heat for 2-3 minutes until transparent. Add the garlic and ginger and cook for 3 minutes. Add the spices (curry, turmeric and tandoori powder, cloves, mustard seeds and garam masala) and cook dry until singed. Add beef pieces, let spices cover them and cook for 5 minutes. Add a few cups of water, peppers and tomato puree and cook for 30 minutes or until the meat is cooked to your taste and the sauce reduced to the thickness you prefer. Add salt to taste a few minutes before serving.

Serve with rice or chapati bread and a side salad.

Serving: 4-6   Time: 55 minutes

Mince Curry with Peas

Ingredients

4	tablespoons olive oil
1	teaspoon peppercorns (or coarsely ground black pepper)
2	onions, finely chopped
2	garlic cloves (or 2 heaped teaspoons minced garlic)
1	teaspoon ginger shavings (or 1 teaspoon ground ginger)
1	teaspoon ground coriander
1	tablespoon curry powder
½	teaspoon turmeric
1	heaped tablespoon garam masala
500	grams minced meat
1	cup peas (fresh, frozen or tinned)
1	tin chopped tomatoes
1	cup boiling water
1	tablespoon tomato puree
	Salt

Heat the oil in a pan until hot, add the onions and cook on medium heat for 2-3 minutes until transparent. Add the garlic and ginger and cook for 3 minutes. Add the spices (curry powder, turmeric, garam masala and coriander) and cook dry until singed. Add the mince and cook for 10 minutes or until brown. Add tomatoes, peas, water and tomato puree and cook for 20 minutes. Add salt to taste a few minutes before serving.

Serve with rice or chapati bread.

"Great for Sunday nights!"

Serving: 4-6   Time: 40 minutes

Indian Meatloaf

Ingredients

4	tablespoons olive oil
1	teaspoon ground white pepper
1	onion, finely chopped
2	garlic cloves
	(or 2 heaped teaspoons minced garlic)
1	teaspoon ginger shavings
	(or 1 teaspoon ground ginger)
½	teaspoon mustard seeds
1	teaspoon curry powder
1	teaspoon tandoori powder
1	teaspoon garam masala
½	teaspoon cumin powder
½	teaspoon ground coriander
1	heaped tablespoon tomato puree
250	grams minced beef
250	grams beef sausage meat
1	teaspoon flour
1	egg
½	cup breadcrumbs
1	teaspoon vegemite
2	tablespoons tomato sauce
1	cup boiling water
	Salt

Mix all ingredients except breadcrumbs, vegemite, tomato sauce and water together thoroughly in a large bowl. Pack down in a rectangular tin or dish. Mix the vegemite, tomato sauce and water and pour over meatloaf. Sprinkle with breadcrumbs, cover and bake in oven at 220 C (Gas Mark 6) for 30 minutes. Remove the cover, increase the heat to 225 C (Gas Mark 7) and cook for 15 minutes.

Serve with a salad and vegetarian curry.

Serving: 6-8   Time: 1 hour

Easy Lamb Curry

Ingredients

4	tablespoons olive oil
2	onions, finely chopped
1	clove
2	whole chillies
1	teaspoon peppercorns (or coarsely ground black pepper)
2	garlic cloves (or 2 heaped teaspoons minced garlic)
1	teaspoon ginger shavings (or 1 teaspoon ground ginger)
2	heaped tablespoons tandoori powder
1	heaped tablespoon garam masala
1	tinned chopped tomatoes (or 3 tomatoes, freshly chopped)
2	cups boiling water
2	tablespoons tomato puree
500	grams lamb, cubed
	Salt

Heat the oil in a pan until hot, add the onions, clove and chillies and cook on medium heat for 2-3 minutes until transparent. Add the garlic and ginger and cook for 3 minutes. Add the spices (tandoori powder and garam masala) and cook dry until singed. Add the lamb cubes, let spices cover them and cook for 5 minutes. Add tomatoes, water and tomato puree and bring to the boil. Reduce heat and cook for 45 minutes. If the curry starts sticking to the bottom of the pan, add a little water. Add salt to taste a few minutes before serving.

"The longer it cooks the more the ingredients blend and the better it tastes"

Serve with rice or chapati bread and a side salad.

Other suggestions
- Add cooked potatoes.
- Add chillies with garlic if you want it spicier.
- You can replace lamb with beef.

Serving: 4-6   Time: 1 hour

Rack of Lamb with Masala and Caramelised Onions

Ingredients

Lamb

4	tablespoons olive oil
1	teaspoon ground black pepper
1	teaspoon salt
1	tablespoon lime juice
2	garlic cloves (or 2 heaped teaspoons minced garlic)

Caramelised Onions

2	tablespoons olive oil
10	red onions, sliced
¼	cup brown sugar
1	teaspoon balsamic vinegar

Optional for caramelised onions

½	teaspoon tamarind paste
	Salt to taste

1	heaped teaspoon coriander powder
1	heaped teaspoon chilli powder
1	heaped tablespoon tandoori powder
1	heaped teaspoon garam masala
1	heaped tablespoon tomato puree
1	heaped tablespoon yoghurt
1	tablespoon mint sauce
1	cup breadcrumbs
¼	cup chopped parsley
4-6	racks of lamb

Place all ingredients for the lamb mix except the breadcrumbs and parsley in a bowl and mix thoroughly. Lather the lamb with the mix ensuring it thoroughly covers each rack of lamb. Coat each rack in breadcrumbs and parsley. Place on rack in oven and cook for 40 minutes at 220 C (Gas Mark 6).

Heat the oil in a pan and when hot add the onions and cook for 30 minutes, adding 1 teaspoonful of sugar every 10 minutes. Add vinegar and the remaining sugar and cook for a further 10 minutes.

Serve with sautéed potatoes and rocket and perhaps plum sauce.

Serving: 4-6   Time: 50 minutes

Steak Tikka Masala

Ingredients

4	tablespoons olive oil
2	onions, finely chopped
1	teaspoon coriander seeds or coriander powder
1	teaspoon mustard seeds
1	heaped teaspoon chilli powder or 3 whole green finger chillies
2	garlic cloves (or 2 heaped teaspoons minced garlic)
1	teaspoon ginger shavings (or 1 teaspoon ground ginger)
½	teaspoon nutmeg
1	heaped tablespoon garam masala
1½	tablespoons tandoori powder
4	medium sized steaks, cubed
4	tablespoons tomato puree
	Water
	Salt

Heat the oil in a pan until hot, add the onions and cook on medium heat for 2-3 minutes until transparent. Add the garlic and ginger and cook for 3 minutes. Add the spices (coriander seeds, mustard seeds, nutmeg, garam masala and tandoori powder) and cook dry until singed. Add the steak cubes, cover them in the spices and cook for 5 minutes. Add tomato puree and then add water to just cover the steak pieces. Bring to the boil, reduce heat and cook for ½ hour. Add salt to taste.

Serve with rice or chapati bread and a side salad.

Other suggestions
- Add 1 tablespoon of sugar or honey for a sweeter dish.
- Add 1 tablespoon of cream to make it creamier, or yoghurt to lessen the richness.
- If you prefer more tender meat, you may wish to pre-cook the meat separately before adding it to the spices and sauce.

Serving: 4-6   Time: 40 minutes

Meat Pilau

Ingredients

4	tablespoons olive oil
1	onion, finely chopped
1	clove
3	whole chillies
2	garlic cloves (or 2 heaped teaspoons minced garlic)
1	teaspoon ginger shavings (or 1 teaspoon ground ginger)
1	teaspoon black pepper
1	teaspoon curry powder
1	teaspoon garam masala
1	teaspoon turmeric
500	grams lamb, cubed
3	tomatoes, freshly chopped
3	cups basmati rice, washed
3	cups boiling water
1	teaspoon butter
1	tablespoon salt
¼	cup chopped fresh coriander

"Very Popular and a Meal in One"

Heat the oil in a pan. Sear and pre-cook the lamb for 15 minutes then remove from the pan. Reheat the oil and when hot add the onion and cook for 2 minutes. Add the clove and whole chillies and cook for 1 minute, being careful not to break the chillies. Add the garlic, ginger, spices (pepper, curry powder, garam masala and turmeric), and tomatoes and cook for 5 minutes. Add the lamb, basmati rice and salt and mix together cooking on high for 2 minutes until lamb and rice are coated in spices. Add boiling water and butter and bring to the boil. Cover, reduce heat to low and cook for 30 minutes.

Serve with sprinkled coriander.

Serving: 4-6   Time: 55 minutes

Roasted Spiced Leg of Lamb

Ingredients

4	tablespoons olive oil
1	teaspoon ground white pepper
1	teaspoon salt
2	garlic cloves
	(or 2 heaped teaspoons minced garlic)
1	heaped tablespoon chilli powder
½	teaspoon mustard powder
½	teaspoon coriander powder
1	heaped tablespoon tandoori powder
1	teaspoon garam masala
1	heaped tablespoon tomato puree
1	heaped tablespoon yoghurt
	Leg of lamb

Place all ingredients in large bowl and mix together thoroughly. Make deep slits in the lamb and lather the lamb in the mixture, also filling the slits.

Cover and cook slowly in the oven to taste. If you prefer the meat well done (when the lamb falls off the bone) cook for 3 hours. If you prefer the lamb rare, cook for 1 hour. Uncover the lamb 10 minutes before serving and cook at 250 C (Gas Mark 9).

Serve with rice, a salad or vegetarian curry.

Serving: 6-8   Time: 1-3 hours

Curried Kidneys

Ingredients

4	tablespoons olive oil
2	onions, finely chopped
1	teaspoon mustard seeds
4	whole chillies
1	teaspoon peppercorns (or coarsely ground black pepper)
2	garlic cloves (or 2 heaped teaspoons minced garlic)
1	heaped tablespoon tandoori powder
1	heaped tablespoon garam masala
1	teaspoon ground coriander
2	cups boiling water
2	tablespoons tomato puree
500	grams kidneys
	Salt

Heat the oil in a pan until hot, add the onions, mustard seeds and chillies and cook on medium heat for 2-3 minutes until transparent. Add the garlic and cook for 3 minutes. Add the spices (tandoori powder, garam masala and ground coriander) and cook dry until singed. Add the kidneys, cover them in the spices and cook for 5 minutes. Add water and tomato puree and bring to the boil. Reduce heat and cook for 25 minutes. If the curry starts sticking to the bottom of the pan, add a little water. Add salt to taste a few minutes before serving.

Serve with rice or chapati bread and a side salad.

Serving: 4-6   Time: 45 minutes

Lamb Saag

Ingredients

4	tablespoons olive oil
1	teaspoon peppercorns (or coarsely ground black pepper)
1	onion, finely chopped
2	garlic cloves (or 2 heaped teaspoons minced garlic)
1	teaspoon ginger shavings (or 1 teaspoon ground ginger)
1	teaspoon coriander seeds
1	teaspoon cumin seeds
1	tablespoon curry powder
1	heaped tablespoon tandoori powder
1	heaped tablespoon garam masala
2	heaped tablespoons tomato puree
500	grams lamb, cubed
250	grams frozen or tinned spinach
2	cups boiling water
	Salt

Heat the oil in a pan. Sear and pre-cook the lamb for 20 minutes then remove from the pan and set aside. Reheat the oil and when hot add the onions and cook for 2-3 minutes until transparent. Add the pepper, garlic and ginger and cook for 3 minutes. Add the spices (coriander and cumin seeds, tandoori powder, curry powder and garam masala) and cook dry until singed. Add the lamb and cook for 10 minutes (adding water if it becomes too dry). Add water, spinach and tomato puree and cook for 15 minutes. Add salt to taste a few minutes before serving.

Serve with rice or chapati bread and a side salad.

Serving: 4-6   Time: 55 minutes

Lamb Chops and Tomato Curry

Ingredients

4   tablespoons olive oil
1   teaspoon peppercorns
     (or coarsely ground black pepper)
2   onions, finely chopped
2   garlic cloves
     (or 2 heaped teaspoons minced garlic)
2   cloves
2   whole green finger chillies
1   heaped tablespoon tandoori powder
1   heaped tablespoon garam masala
2   heaped tablespoons tomato puree
500 grams chops
4   tomatoes, chopped into wedges
2   cups water
Salt

Optional

½ teaspoon cumin seeds
1 teaspoon ground coriander

"Add some more water ten minutes before serving if you do not want the curry to be too dry"

Grill chops for 5 minutes on each side to sear meat. Heat the oil in a pan until hot, add the onions and cook on medium heat for 2-3 minutes until transparent. Add the cloves, garlic, chillies (and optional ingredients) and cook for 3 minutes. Add the spices (tandoori powder and garam masala) and cook dry until singed. Add the tomatoes and chops, cover them in the spices and cook for a 5 minutes. Add a few cups of water and tomato puree and cook for ½ hour or until the meat is cooked to your taste and the sauce reduced to the thickness you prefer. Add salt to taste a few minutes before serving.

Serve with rice or chapati bread and a side salad.

Serving: 4-6   Time: 55 minutes

Venison Loaf with Baked Egg

Ingredients

4	tablespoons olive oil
1	teaspoon ground white pepper
2	onions, finely chopped
2	heaped teaspoons minced garlic
1	teaspoon ginger shavings (or 1 teaspoon ground ginger)
1	teaspoon mustard seeds
1	tablespoon tandoori powder
1	teaspoon garam masala
1	teaspoon cumin powder
1	teaspoon ground coriander
2	heaped tablespoons tomato puree
500	grams venison sausage meat
3	eggs
	Salt

Mix all ingredients (except 2 of the eggs) thoroughly in a large bowl. Pack mixture down in a large tin or dish. Cover and bake in oven at 220 C, (Gas Mark 6) for 45 minutes.

Remove dish from oven and break 2 eggs over the top of the venison loaf and place under the grill for 3 minutes until eggs are baked or the whites firm.

Serve with salad and chips.

Serving: 6-8   Time: 1 hour

SEAFOOD DISHES

Easy Prawn Curry

Ingredients

4	tablespoons olive oil
1	onion, finely chopped
2	garlic cloves (or 2 heaped teaspoons minced garlic)
1	teaspoon ginger shavings (or 1 teaspoon ground ginger)
1	heaped tablespoon curry powder
1½	tablespoons turmeric
2	tablespoons lemon juice
500	grams fresh or thawed prawns Salt

Heat the oil in a pan until hot, add the onions and cook on medium heat for 2-3 minutes until transparent. Add the garlic and ginger and cook for 3 minutes. Add the spices (curry powder and turmeric) and lemon juice and cook for 2 minutes. Add the prawns and cook for 5 minutes. Add water to just cover the prawns. Bring to the boil, reduce the heat and cook for 10 minutes. Add salt to taste.

Serve with rice or chapati bread and a side salad.

Other suggestions
- Add coconut milk to create a creamier and different flavour.
- Sprinkle with parsley before serving.

Serving: 4-6   Time: 30 minutes

Seafood Delight

Ingredients

4	tablespoons olive oil
1	tablespoon butter
2	onions, finely chopped
1	teaspoon peppercorns (or coarsely ground black pepper)
2	garlic cloves (or 2 heaped teaspoons minced garlic)
1	teaspoon ginger shavings (or 1 teaspoon ground ginger)
1	heaped tablespoon curry powder
1	heaped tablespoon turmeric
½	teaspoon garam masala
½	teaspoon cumin seeds
1	tablespoon lime juice
200	grams prawns
200	grams fish fillets (cod is very tasty)
100	grams scallops
1	cup seafood stock
	Salt

Heat the oil in a pan until hot, add the onions and cook on medium heat for 2-3 minutes until transparent. Add the garlic and ginger and cook for 3 minutes. Add the spices (pepper, curry powder, turmeric, garam masala and cumin seeds) and lime juice and cook for 3 minutes. Add seafood, let spices cover them and cook for 5 minutes. Add water and stock to just cover the seafood. Bring to the boil, reduce heat and cook for 15 minutes. Add salt to taste.

Serve with rice or chapati bread and a side salad.

Other suggestions
- Add mussels or salmon to enrich the flavour.
- Sprinkle with finely chopped spring onions before serving.

Serving: 4-6   Time: 30 minutes

Spicy Sardines

Ingredients

1	tablespoon butter
2	spring onions, finely chopped
½	cup green peppercorns
1	teaspoon ground white pepper
1	teaspoon minced garlic
1	teaspoon minced ginger
1	tablespoon chilli flakes
1	teaspoon lemon peel shavings
3	sardines
1	cup seafood stock
1	cup white wine
	Salt to taste

Heat the butter slowly in a large pan. When melted, add the spring onions and peppercorns and cook on a medium heat for 2-3 minutes until transparent. Add the pepper, garlic, ginger, chilli flakes and lemon shavings and cook for 3 minutes. Add the sardines, stock and wine. Bring to the boil and simmer for 6 minutes on a medium heat or until sardines are cooked through. Add salt to taste.

Place sardines on a plate and pour sauce over sardines. Garnish with coriander and lemon wedges.

Other suggestions
* Replace sardines with other fish such as seabass.

Serving: 3   Time: 20 minutes

Lobster with Chilli and Lemon

Ingredients

Lobster

1	Large pot of boiling water
4	whole lobsters

Turmeric sauce

2	tablespoons olive oil
1	tablespoon butter
1	clove garlic
1	spring onion, finely chopped
2	tablespoons lemon juice
1	teaspoon ground white pepper
1	tablespoon turmeric
1	teaspoon ground coriander
1	teaspoon dried chilli
½	cup cream
	Salt

Lobsters

Bring to the boil a large pot of water. Place lobsters in boiling water and cook for 8 minutes. Drain lobsters and run under cold water. Set aside until serving.

Chilli and lemon sauce

Heat the olive oil and butter in a pan until hot. Add the garlic, spring onion, lemon juice, pepper, turmeric, coriander and chilli and cook for 2 minutes. Add the cream and cook on low for 5 minutes (do not boil). Add salt to taste and remove from heat until ready to serve.

Serve with limes or lemons and a side salad.

Other suggestions

- This sauce can also be used as a side sauce for other seafood dishes.

Serving: 4   Time: 30 minutes

Cod Curry

Ingredients

4	tablespoons olive oil
2	spring onions, finely chopped
2	garlic cloves
	(or 2 heaped teaspoons minced garlic)
1	teaspoon ginger shavings
	(or 1 teaspoon ground ginger)
1	heaped tablespoon curry powder
1	heaped tablespoon turmeric
2	tablespoons lemon or lime juice
500	grams fresh cod fillets
½	tin chopped tomatoes
2	cups boiling water
¼	cup chopped fresh coriander
	Salt

Heat the oil in a pan until hot, add the spring onions and cook on medium heat for 2-3 minutes until transparent. Add the garlic and ginger and cook for 3 minutes. Add the spices (curry powder and turmeric) and lemon/lime juice and cook for 2 minutes. Add the tomatoes and cook for 10 minutes. Add the fish and water, bring to the boil, reduce the heat and cook for 5 minutes. Add the coriander and cook for 5 minutes or until fish is cooked through. Add salt to taste.

Serve with rice and a side salad.

Other suggestions

- Add coconut milk to create a creamier dish with a different flavour.
- Sprinkle with parsley before serving.

Serving: 4-6   Time: 30 minutes

Indian Fish and Chips

Ingredients

Fish

4	tablespoons olive oil
2	garlic cloves (or 2 heaped teaspoons minced garlic)
1	teaspoon ginger shavings (or 1 teaspoon ground ginger)
1	teaspoon curry powder
1	teaspoon garam masala
1	tablespoon lemon juice
½	tin chopped tomatoes
¼	cup chopped fresh coriander
¼	cup chopped fresh coriander
	2 teaspoons minced garlic
500	grams red mullet fillets, cut into slices
	Salt and pepper

Chips

500	grams potatoes	1	teaspoon turmeric
4	tablespoons olive oil	1	teaspoon chilli powder
1	tablespoon butter	½	tin chopped tomatoes
2	teaspoons minced garlic		Salt

Fish

Heat the oil in a pan until hot, add the garlic, ginger, curry powder and garam masala and cook for 2-3 minutes. Add tomatoes and cook for a further 5 mins. Cover fish in lemon juice and then add to mixture. Cook for a further 6 minutes or until the fish is cooked through. Add the coriander and salt and pepper to taste.

Chips

Cut the potatoes into slices and then boil them until almost cooked and then drain and set aside to dry. Heat the oil and butter in a pan until hot, add garlic, turmeric and chilli powder and cook for 1 minute. Add potatoes and tomatoes and fry in mixture for 5 minutes or until potatoes are cooked through. Add salt to taste.

Serving: 4-6   Time: 45 minutes

Zesty Scallops with Turmeric, Coriander and Lime

Ingredients

Scallops
2   tablespoons butter
500 grams scallops

Turmeric sauce
2   tablespoons olive oil
1   tablespoon butter
2   spring onions, finely chopped
1   teaspoon ground black pepper
1   tablespoon turmeric
1   teaspoon ground cumin powder
1   cup white wine
1   cup chicken stock
2   egg yolks
½   cup cream
    Salt

Coriander and lime juice
1   Bunch fresh coriander
3   tablespoons lime juice
1   teaspoon chilli powder
    Salt and pepper to taste

Coriander and lime juice
Mix all ingredients and blend until smooth.

Scallops
Heat butter in a pan until hot, add cleaned scallops and cook for 7 minutes.

While the scallops are cooking, make the turmeric sauce. Heat the olive oil and butter in a pan until hot. Add the spring onions, pepper, turmeric and cumin and cook for 1 minute. Add the white wine and stock and bring to the boil. Blend mixture until smooth. Reduce heat and add the egg yolks and cream, and cook on low heat for 5 minutes (do not boil). Add salt to taste and remove from heat until ready to serve.

Serve with rocket and rice.

Other suggestions
•   Replace cream with coconut cream in the turmeric sauce for a more exotic flavour.

Serving: 4-6   Time: 30 minutes

Salmon Fish Cakes

Ingredients

1	tablespoon olive oil
1	onion, finely chopped
1	teaspoon minced garlic
½	teaspoon chilli flakes
½	cup chopped fresh coriander
6	cups mashed potatoes
500	grams salmon, flaked
3	cups golden breadcrumbs
2	eggs, whisked
½	cup flour
	Salt and pepper to taste

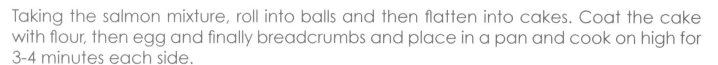

Combine the onion, garlic, chilli flakes, coriander, potatoes, salmon and 1 cup of breadcrumbs into a large bowl. Sprinkle the flour onto a large plate, sprinkle the remaining breadcrumbs onto another large plate and pour the eggs into a dipping bowl. Heat olive oil in a pan.

Taking the salmon mixture, roll into balls and then flatten into cakes. Coat the cake with flour, then egg and finally breadcrumbs and place in a pan and cook on high for 3-4 minutes each side.

Serve with rocket and spinach and raita.

Other suggestions
- You can also grill or bake the fish cakes.

Serving: 4-6   Time: 45 minutes

DESSERTS

Coconut Ice

Ingredients

3	cups icing sugar
30	grams melted butter
½	cup milk
¾	cup desiccated coconut
2	drops pink food colouring

Sift icing sugar into a medium sized pot. Add the milk and butter and place on a low heat, whisking gently until sugar is dissolved. Slowly bring to the boil and simmer until it has the texture of a soft ball. Add the coconut and remove from heat. Let it stand for 10-15 minutes until cool but not thickened. Halve the mixture. Add the colouring to one half of the mixture and beat until thick. Place in a deep square cake tin. Beat the other half of the mixture until thick and spread it on top of the pink mixture. Allow to cool and cut into cubes.

Serving: 10-12   Time: 40 minutes

Banana Cake

Ingredients

Cake

130 grams butter
¾   cup sugar
1   pinch of salt
2   eggs
2   cups mashed ripe bananas
1   teaspoon baking soda
2   tablespoons milk
2   cups plain flour
1   teaspoon baking powder

Icing

2½   cups icing sugar
1½   tablespoons softened butter
3-4 tablespoons boiling water

Cake

Heat butter slowly on low heat and when melted, add sugar. Whisk together until creamy and light. Whisk in eggs one at a time. Add banana and mix together. Heat milk, add baking soda then add to banana mixture in a seperate bowl. Sift flour and baking powder into mixture and add salt. Place in (greased or Teflon) cake or loaf tin and bake at 180 degrees (Gas Mark 4) for 55 minutes. Remove from oven, leave to stand in tin for 15 minutes and then turn on to a rack to cool.

Icing

Combine icing sugar and butter in large bowl. Add water, 1 tablespoon at a time, to the mixture stirring continuously until mixture is smooth and creamy. (Be careful not to add too much water.)

When the cake is cold, cover with white icing and sprinkle with icing sugar.

Serving: 10-12   Time: 1 hour 10 minutes

Mango Eton Mess

Ingredients

4   meringue nests
2   mangos
300 ml whipping cream
1   teaspoon mint leaves

Break the meringue nests into crumbs into a large bowl. Chop the mango into small cubes and add to the meringue crumbs. Whip cream and add to the mixture. Serve in separate bowls and sprinkle mint on top.

Other suggestions
- You can try other exotic fruit as an alternative.
- Kiwifruit makes a good substitute when exotic fruit is out of season.

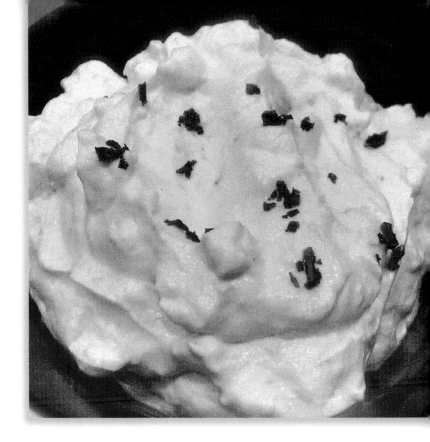

Serving: 4-6   Time: 15 minutes

Kiwifruit Sorbet

Ingredients

6	kiwifruit
½	cup castor sugar
1	cup water
2	egg whites

Peel kiwifruit and blend into a puree. Heat the water in a small pot over a low heat. Add sugar and whisk gently until all of the sugar is dissolved. Remove from heat and let it stand to cool. When the mixture reaches room temperature, fold pureed kiwifruit into the mixture. Pour into a freezer-proof container and place in freezer for 2 hours or until the top is starting to freeze. Remove from freezer and fold in egg whites and beat for 10 minutes. Put the sorbet into freezer-proof serving dishes or glasses, freeze for 2 hours then serve.

Other suggestions
- If you prefer a less sweet sorbet, add 1 tablespoon lime juice and 1 teaspoon of grated lemon rind.

Serving: 4   Time: 30 minutes (not including 4 hours freezing time)

Lychee Trifle

Ingredients
7	gram sachet of fruit jelly crystals
¼	pint boiling water
¾	pint cool water
1 ½	cups peeled lychees, preferably fresh. (If using tinned lychees, drain fruit.)
2	cups ready-made custard
400	ml whipping cream
1	tablespoon coloured sprinkles

Place lychees in large deep serving dish. Put jelly crystals into a heat-proof measuring jug. Pour boiling water over jelly crystals, whisking to dissolve jelly crystals. When dissolved, add cool water. Pour jelly mixture over lychees and place dish in fridge for 2 hours or until jelly has completely set. Remove from fridge and cover jelly with custard. Beat whipping cream and cover the custard. Place in fridge until ready to serve, covering with sprinkles or grated chocolate just before serving.

Other suggestions
- You can replace the lychees with other preferred or seasonal fruit.
- If you enjoy alcoholic jelly replace one cup of the cool water with champagne.

Serving: 8   Time: 25 minutes (not including 2 hours cooling time)

Zahra's Enchanting Pears

Ingredients

4	pears
4	teaspoons brown sugar
1	teaspoon ground nutmeg
3	teaspoons ground cinnamon
2	teaspoons ground mixed spice
4	tablespoons golden syrup

Pre-heat the oven to 190 C (gas mark 5). Halve the pears and remove all seeds. Sprinkle the pears with the nutmeg, cinnamon and mixed spice and then pour the golden syrup equally over the pears. Place in the oven for 20 minutes. Remove from heat and sprinkle brown sugar over the pears and place under grill for 5 minutes or until sugar crisps.

Serve warm with sponge or madeira cake.

Serving: 4-6   Time: 30 minutes

Coconut Ice-Cream

Ingredients
250 ml milk
1   tin coconut cream
400 ml double cream
100 grams desiccated coconut
1   cup castor sugar

Combine the milk and coconut cream and blend for 3 minutes. Add the cream, coconut and sugar and blend for 3 minutes. Pour into an ice cream container or freezer-proof dish and freeze for 10 hours or until ice-cream hardens.

Serving: 10   Time: 20 minutes (not including 10 hours freezing time)

Seline's Chocolate Banana's

Ingredients

Bananas

25 grams butter
40 grams brown sugar
1   tablespoon golden syrup
½   teaspoon cinnamon
½   teaspoon ground mixed spices
1   tablespoon lemon juice
4   large peeled bananas

Chocolate sauce

100 grams milk chocolate
2   tablespoons of golden syrup
15 grams butter
2   tablespoons water

Bananas

Pre-heat the oven to 200 C (gas mark 6). Cut 4 rectangle sheets of tin foil (approximately 30cm x 20 cm). In a small pan heat the butter over low heat until softened and stir until creamy. Add cinnamon, mixed spice and syrup to the creamy mixture. Cover the bananas in lemon juice and place them onto the tin foil. Pour mixture over bananas. Pour golden syrup and lemon juice over bananas and seal foil before placing in the oven for 20 minutes.

Sauce

While the bananas are cooking make the chocolate sauce. Heat butter in a pan slowly until melted. Add water and golden syrup and stir until mixed. Add chocolate and stir until a smooth mixture.

Remove bananas from oven and serve with chocolate sauce over the bananas or to the side.

Serving: 4-6   Time: 30 minutes

ACCOMPANIMENTS

Rice

What type of rice
As a rule, Basmati rice is always used for Indian cooking. It is lighter and smaller than most other rice and more enjoyable for heavier dishes such as curries.

How to prepare rice
It is important that rice is always rinsed well in order to remove all the starch. Place your rice in a sieve and run under cold water for a few minutes, shaking the rice so all pieces are thoroughly washed. Once the water is no longer milky let it stand until you are ready to put in the pot. For rice cooking one cup of rice will require one cup of water. So if you need 3 cups of rice you will also need 3 cups of water. In a pot put the amount of water you require and add a teaspoon of salt and a teaspoon of butter (or olive oil).

How to cook rice
Put your pot of water on the hob to boil and once boiled add the rice. Bring back to the boil and let it boil for 1 minute and then cover the pot and turn to low until the rice is cooked. For 2 cups of rice this should take 20 minutes, for more cups it will take some more time. Rice can be quite difficult to cook for the novice, but once you find your own way it can become second nature.

Suggestions
Rice is quite easy to experiment with so feel free to add a teaspoon of turmeric in the water, or grate a couple of tablespoons of vegetables (such as carrots) to add to the rice. You can also replace water with coconut milk (not cream) to create quite a different rice dish.

Chapati Bread

Chapati (also known as Roti)
Personally, I only make chapatis when I have ample time, this is because it takes my mother-in-law 5 minutes to make 100 and often takes me 100 minutes to make 5. They are quite difficult to make and you need utensils such as a chapati rolling pin (which is much thinner than a baking one) and many people now use a chapati machine which flattens the chapati into a nice round flat circle. You also usually require a chapati skittle or griddle pan which is very thick and flat. Another reason I prefer to buy them is that it can be difficult to buy chapati flour from the local supermarket, so unless you are doing a stock up in bulk you cannot always purchase it 'on the day' so often I have to substitute the chapati flour for wholemeal flour.

To make chapatis you will need
250 g chapati flour (but can be substituted
         with wholemeal flour)
1   tablespoon olive oil
150 ml water

In a large bowl put the flour and add the oil bit by bit until the oil has mixed with all the flour. Add small portions of the water at a time and knead into the flour to make it into dough. Turn the griddle onto high and heat up while you roll your dough into chapatis. Take a small ball from the dough and start flattening out on a flat surface (dusting with the flour) until your chapati is round and flat.

Place each chapati onto the griddle for 30 seconds each side. If you want to brown the chapatis up you will need to place it over a naked flame on the hob for a few seconds each side. Be sure to use tongs to not burn yourself. Once cooked, place on a plate and cover them with a cloth. Once you have cooked your chapatis, cover the plate with tin foil to keep warm.

Other suggestions
•   You can also replace chapatis with Naan bread or pita bread.

The Pink Stuff

Ingredients
2   cups natural yoghurt
½   cup finely chopped onion
½   cup finely chopped cucumber
3   heaped tablespoons chilli powder

Combine all ingredients

Time: 10 minutes

"One is cooling – for those who prefer less spice – while the other is incredibly spicy and makes a fantastic accompaniment to those who like their food very hot!"

Easy Cool Raita

Ingredients
2   cups natural yoghurt
½   cup finely chopped onion
½   cup finely chopped cucumber
2   tablespoons mint sauce

Combine all ingredients

Time: 10 minutes

Effortless Sweet Chilli and Yoghurt

Ingredients
1   cup natural yoghurt
½   cup sweet chilli sauce

Combine all ingredients

Time: 1 minute

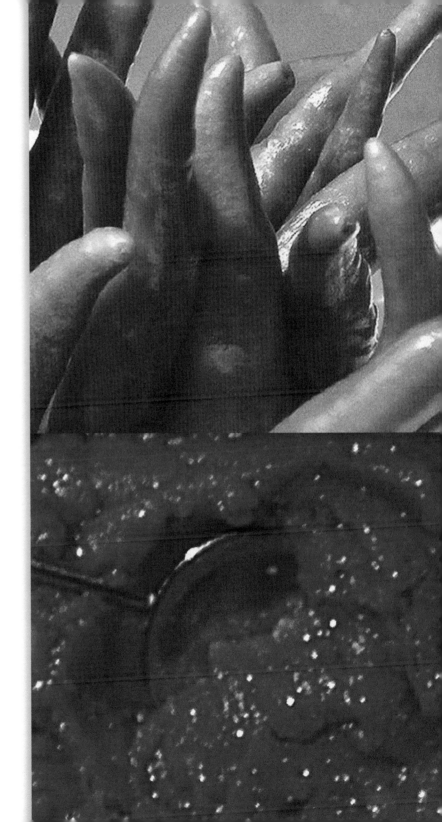

Simple Tomato and Chilli Sauce

Ingredients
1   cup tomato sauce
2   tablespoons chilli powder

Combine all ingredients

Time: 1 minute

Fried Chillies

Ingredients
4   tablespoons vegetable oil
3   cups green finger chillies
1   tablespoon cumin seeds
1   tablespoon mustard seeds

Heat the oil in a pan and when hot, add cumin and mustard seeds, and then add the chillies. Keeping the heat on high, cover and cook, shaking the pan continuously so the chillies singe but do not burn.

After 8 minutes, set aside on a tissue or kitchen towel and let chillies drain.
Serve as an accompaniment to any dish.

Time: 10 minutes

Bullet Chillies

Ingredients

4   tablespoons vegetable oil
2   garlic cloves
     (or 2 teaspoons of crushed garlic)
3   handfuls of bullet chillies, slit and seeded
½   tin chopped tomatoes
     Salt to taste

Heat the oil in a pan and when hot, add the garlic and cook for one minute. Add the chillies and cook for a further 3 minutes. Add the tomatoes, cover and cook for 5 minutes on medium heat.

Serve as an accompaniment to any dish.

Time: 15 minutes

How to cook for
20 people in less than
60 minutes for less than £30

The great thing about Indian cooking is that you really can make several curries at the same time because most curries have the same base and similar ingredients. Whether you are cooking for two, ten or twenty there is often a similar amount of time involved. It is always a good idea to make the more simple recipes and those that are not too expensive.

It is imperative that you have all the necessary ingredients and all the utensils that you will need in front of you before you start cooking.

With twenty people around, remember that people will be moving about. It is best not to have anything too complicated (such as masala chops) for them to eat while socialising. Sociable food is what you need – something not too difficult to eat when standing up or with plates on laps.

Below are a couple of examples for what I cook for twenty people. I usually include one meat and one or two vegetable curries. These examples provide a variety of food that caters for vegetarians and aims to please everyone. They are organised to be distinct and diverse in flavour although similar ingredients are used. If you want to tighten your budget further, just make vegetarian dishes!

The following menus and costing demonstrate how you can make a feast on a good budget. The listings are Tesco price-matched in November 2010 so many of the ingredients (such as the fruit) are out of season and will be cheaper (or more expensive) at different times of the year. You can save a lot more money if you shop for specials or buy in bulk. Each ingredient you will need is listed here, including salt, pepper and oil, and is priced for those starting from scratch.

Afterwards you should still have some change from your £30, some left-over ingredients and hopefully some left-over curry for the next day.

Each recipe in the book caters for up to 6 people. You will need to double the quantities for the curries because doubling three curries is cooking for at least twenty-four people. You and your guests should have more than enough food. Note that not everyone eats dessert, particularly after a curry.

Some of the recipes below have minor changes (for example, mango has been replaced with kiwifruit) although the essential ingredients remain the same and some ingredients have been replaced for cost reasons. Also, when cooking in large quantities some of the measurements will change slightly so the recipes below should be followed below.

These menu examples are designed to show that it is relatively easy to cook these within an hour, often with spare time in between to clear up and get on with other things. It sounds like more of a multi-task than it actually is. It is not a marathon or a race against the clock. Take your time; it'll all work out in the end...

Menu One: Easy Chicken Curry, Spinach and Paneer Curry and Chickpea and Sweet Corn Curry Served with Rice. Lychee Trifle

Ingredients you will need	Price per item	Product Description and quantity	Total price
EASY CHICKEN CURRY – FOLLOW RECIPE ON PAGE 44			
¼ cup olive oil	£1.84	Tesco olive oil 500 ml	£1.84
4 onions	£0.85	Cooking onions 1 kg x 2	£1.70
1 teaspoon black peppercorns	£1.07	Whole black peppercorns 100 g	£1.07
4 garlic cloves	£0.24	1 garlic bulb	£0.24
4 teaspoons ginger shavings	£0.68	1 piece large ginger root	£0.68
4 heaped tablespoons turmeric	£0.99	Ground turmeric 100 g x 2	£1.98
2 heaped tablespoons garam masala	£0.77	Garam masala 38 g x 3	£2.31
2 tins chopped tomatoes	£0.33	Tinned chopped tomatoes 400 g x 2	£0.66
1 kg chicken thighs	£3.62	Tesco pack thighs 900-1100 g	£3.62
1 tablespoon salt	£0.23	Tesco Value table salt 1 kg	£0.23
		Total cost:	**£14.33**
SPINACH AND PANEER CURRY – FOLLOW RECIPE ON PAGE 29			
¼ cup olive oil		PA	
2 onions		PA	
1 teaspoon black peppercorns		PA	
2 teaspoons chilli powder	£0.67	Tesco hot chilli powder 50 g	£0.67
4 garlic cloves		PA	
2 teaspoons ginger shavings		PA	
2 heaped tablespoons curry powder	£0.70	Curry powder 80 g	£0.70
1 teaspoon turmeric		PA	
2 heaped tablespoons garam masala		PA	
1 tin chopped tomatoes	£0.33	Tinned chopped tomatoes 400 g x 2	£0.66
3 heaped tablespoons tomato puree	£0.25	Tin tomato puree 142 g	£0.25
4 tins leaf spinach	£0.53	Tin leaf spinach 380 g x 4	£2.12
60 g paneer cheese	£1.40	Paneer cheese 227 g	£1.40
1 tablespoon salt		PA	
		Total cost:	**£5.80**

PA=Purchased above in previous recipe

CHICKPEA AND SWEET CORN CURRY – FOLLOW RECIPE ON PAGE 32

¼ cup olive oil		PA	
4 onions		PA	
1 teaspoon peppercorns		PA	
2 teaspoons chilli powder		PA	
2 garlic cloves		PA	
2 cloves	£0.65	Tesco whole cloves 35 g	£0.65
2 teaspoons ginger shavings		PA	
2 teaspoons curry powder		PA	
2 heaped tablespoons turmeric		PA	
2 teaspoons garam masala		PA	
1½ tins chopped tomatoes	£0.33	Tesco chopped tomatoes 400 g x 2	£0.66
2 tins cooked chickpeas (drained)	£0.48	Tesco chickpea 400 g x 2	£0.96
2 tins sweet corn (drained)	£0.32	Tesco natural sweet corn 200 g x 2	£0.64
1 tablespoon of salt		PA	
		Total cost:	**£2.91**
5 cups basmati rice	£1.47	Basmati rice 1kg	£1.47

DESSERT - LYCHEE TRIFLE – FOLLOW RECIPE ON PAGE 93

14 g fruit jelly crystals	£0.36	Raspberry jelly crystals 135 g	£0.36
½ pint boiling water			
1½ pints cool water			
1 tin lychees	£1.35	Lychees in syrup 425 g	£1.35
4 cups readymade custard	£0.24	Ready to serve custard 396 g x 2	£0.48
800ml whipping cream	£0.85	Whipping cream 300 ml x 3	£2.55
Chocolate sprinkles	£0.30	Tesco milk chocolate 100 g	£0.30
		Total cost:	**£5.04**

TOTAL COST OF MEAL	**£29.55**

Approximate Times

Easy Chicken Curry	50 minutes
Spinach and Paneer Curry	30 minutes
Chick Peas and Sweet Corn Curry	30 minutes
Lychee Trifle	25 minutes (plus 2 hours' cooling time)

PA=Purchased above in previous recipe

Remember to have all your ingredients to hand before you start cooking.

To start the hour, start heating three pans – one for each of the curries – on the hob at the same time. Add oil to each and, when hot, add the appropriate quantity of onions to each at the same time, then the garlic and ginger and the rest of the spices for each dish. Keep stirring all of them while they cook, adding water when needed.

Once the main ingredients have been added, prepare the rice by washing it and start it cooking. Add any remaining ingredients to your curries while they simmer and cook and turn your attention to the dessert by first whipping the cream. Your rice should now be boiling so keep it covered and be sure to turn it down to low.

Keep stirring your curries and then remove the jellied lychees from the fridge, pour on the custard, then the cream, coat with chocolate sprinkles and put back into the fridge. Once the vegetarian curries are cooked, remove them from the hob and set aside until you need to reheat them for serving. Although cooked after 50 minutes, the chicken can be left to simmer for up to a couple of hours on a very low heat to let the flavours continue to combine and the meat fall off the bone. (Remember to stir frequently and add water when needed.) Or you can serve it straight away, removing any bones first if you prefer. You may even have time to set the table and get yourself ready in this time-frame as well!

Menu Two: Chicken Tikka Masala with Potato and Egg Curry and Vegetarian Pilau and to finish with Kiwifruit Eton Mess

Ingredients you will need	Price per item	Product Description and quantity	Total price
CHICKEN TIKKA MASALA – FOLLOW RECIPE ON PAGE 45			
½ cup olive oil	£1.84	Tesco olive oil 500 ml	£1.84
4 onions	£0.85	Cooking onions 1 kg	£0.85
4 garlic cloves	£1.07	1 garlic bulb	£1.07
2 teaspoons ginger shavings	£0.24	1 piece large root ginger	£0.24
2 teaspoons coriander powder	£0.40	Ground coriander 36 g	£0.40
2 heaped teaspoons chilli powder	£0.67	Tesco hot chilli powder 50 g	£0.67
2 teaspoons nutmeg	£1.16	Tesco ground nutmeg 52 g	£1.16
2 tablespoons garam masala	£0.77	Garam masala powder 38 g x 2	£1.44
3 tablespoons tandoori powder	£0.70	Tandoori curry powder 80 g x 2	£1.40
1 kg chicken thighs	£3.62	Tesco pack thighs 900-1100 g	£3.62
4 tablespoons tomato puree	£0.25	1 tin tomato puree 142 g x 2	£0.50
Water			
1 tablespoon salt	£0.23	Tesco value table salt 1 kg	£0.23
		Total cost:	**£13.49**
POTATO AND EGG CURRY – FOLLOW RECIPE ON PAGE 28			
½ cup olive oil		PA	
3 finely chopped onions		PA	
1 teaspoon peppercorns	£1.07	Tesco whole black peppercorns	£1.07
2 garlic cloves		PA	
2 teaspoons ginger shavings		PA	
2 heaped tablespoons curry powder	£1.10	Tesco mild curry powder 80 g	£1.10
2 heaped tablespoons turmeric	£0.99	Turmeric powder 100 g	£0.99
1 kg cooked new potatoes	£1.39	Baby new potatoes 1 kg	£1.39
12 hard boiled eggs cut into halves	£1.45	Tesco eggs (box of 15)	£1.45
1½ tablespoons salt		PA	
		Total cost:	**£6.00**

PA=Purchased above in previous recipe

VEGETARIAN PILAU – FOLLOW RECIPE ON PAGE 40

½	cup olive oil		PA	
1	onion		PA	
2	cloves	£0.65	Tesco whole cloves 35 g	£0.65
2	garlic cloves		PA	
2	teaspoons ginger shavings		PA	
2	teaspoons peppercorns		PA	
2	teaspoons curry powder		PA	
1	teaspoon garam masala		PA	
1	teaspoon turmeric		PA	
900 g	mixed vegetables	£0.33	Tesco mixed vegetables 907 g	£0.33
2	red onions	£0.20	Loose red onions x 2	£0.40
6	chopped tomatoes	£0.85	Tesco salad tomatoes 6 pack	£0.85
6	cups washed basmati rice	£1.47	Basmati rice 1 kg	£1.47
6	cups boiling water			
1	tablespoon olive oil for rice water		PA	
1 ½	tablespoon salt		PA	
			Total cost:	**£3.70**

DESSERT – KIWIFRUIT ETON MESS (SUBSTITUTED FROM MANGO) – FOLLOW RECIPE ON PAGE 91

12	meringue nests	£0.98	Tesco 8 meringue nest pack x 2	£1.96
8	kiwifruit	£1.00	Pre-pack 8 kiwifruit	£1.00
300ml	whipping cream	£0.85	Whipping cream 300 ml x 3	£2.55
2	teaspoon mint leaves	£0.79	Fresh mint 30 g	£0.79
			Total cost:	**£6.30**

TOTAL COST OF MEAL £29.49

Approximate Times

Chicken Tikka Masala	40 minutes
Potato and Egg Curry	40 minutes
Vegetarian Pilau	35 minutes
Kiwifruit Eton Mess	15 minutes

PA=Purchased above in previous recipe

To start the hour put the eggs in a large pot of cold water and turn on high to bring to the boil. Start heating 3 pans – one for each of the curries – on the hob at the same time. Add oil to each and, when hot, add the appropriate quantity of onions to each at the same time, then the garlic and ginger and the rest of the ingredients for each dish (which should be to hand). Keep stirring all of them while they cook, adding water when needed. Turn the eggs down when boiling and after 5 minutes remove from hob, drain hot water and refill with cold water so the eggs can cool down to peel.

Prepare the rice by washing it and ensure you have boiling water to hand. Once the base of the pilau and all its contents are cooked, put the boiling water and rice, salt and oil into the pot, cover and bring to the boil. Peel the eggs and place in the potato and egg curry. Once the rice is boiling, cover and turn to low until cooked (approx 30 minutes). Continue to stir curries and add water if they become too dry. You now have time to prepare your dessert.

Menu Three: Venison Loaf with Baked Egg and Mixed Vegetarian Curry served with Chapatis and to finish with Fresh Sliced Pineapple

Ingredients you will need	Price per item	Product Description and quantity	Total price
VENISON LOAF WITH BAKED EGG – FOLLOW RECIPE ON PAGE 74			
2 tablespoons olive oil	£1.84	Tesco olive oil 500 ml	£1.84
2 teaspoons ground white pepper	£0.38	Saxa white pepper 25 g	£0.38
4 onions	£0.85	Cooking onions 1 kg	£0.85
4 cloves crushed garlic	£0.24	1 Garlic bulb	£0.24
2 teaspoons ginger shavings	£0.68	1 piece large root ginger	£0.68
2 teaspoons mustard seeds	£0.63	Mustard seeds 70 g	£0.63
2 tablespoons tandoori powder	£0.70	Tandoori curry powder 80 g	£0.70
2 teaspoons garam masala	£0.77	Garam masala 38 g	£0.77
2 teaspoons ground cumin	£0.40	Ground cumin 43 g	£0.40
2 teaspoons ground coriander	£0.40	Ground coriander 36 g	£0.40
4 heaped tablespoons tomato puree	£0.25	1 tin tomato puree 142 g x 2	£0.50
900g venison sausage meat	£2.99	Pack 6 Venison sausages 300 g x 3	£8.97
6 eggs	£0.89	Tesco eggs (box of 15)	£0.89
1 tablespoon salt	£0.23	Tesco value table salt 1 kg	£0.23
		Total cost:	**£14.33**
MIXED VEGETABLE CURRY – FOLLOW RECIPE ON PAGE 31			
¼ cup olive oil		PA	
5 onions		PA	
4 garlic cloves		PA	
2 teaspoons ginger shavings		PA	
1 teaspoon white pepper		PA	
2 teaspoons chilli powder	£0.67	Tesco hot chilli powder 50 g	£0.67
3 heaped tablespoons turmeric	£0.99	Turmeric powder 100 g	£0.99
3 teaspoons garam masala		PA	
2 teaspoons ground cumin powder		PA	
2 tins chopped tomatoes	£0.33	1 tin chopped tomatoes 400 g x 2	£0.66
½ cauliflower	£0.76	Tesco cauliflower	£0.76
500 g new potatoes	£0.64	Tesco tin new potatoes 800 g	£0.64
500 g mixed vegetables with peppers	£1.36	Mixed veg with red peppers 1 kg	£1.36

PA=Purchased above in previous recipe

8 cups of water		PA	
1½ tablespoons salt		**Total cost:**	**£5.08**

SALAD

Iceberg Lettuce	£0.85	Iceberg lettuce x 2	£1.70
Red onion	£0.20	Loose red onion x 2	£0.40
Cucumber	£0.70	Whole cucumber	£0.70
Tomato	£0.13	Tomato on the Vine Loose x 3	£0.39
		Total cost:	**£3.19**
Chapatis, halved	£0.99	Pataks plain chapatis 6 x 3	£2.97

DESSERT – SLICED PINEAPPLE

Pineapple	£1.25	Gold Pineapple	£1.25
		Total cost:	**£1.25**

TOTAL COST OF MEAL £29.97

Approximate Times

Venison with Baked Egg	60 minutes
Mixed Vegetable Curry	40 minutes

This menu plan takes a little more time to cook but there is less preparation involved. As there is not a lot to do during the cooking, you will have ample time to prepare the salad, slice the pineapple, clean up, set the table and so on while the curries are cooking.

To start the hour, have a pan on the hob for the vegetarian curry and a large bowl ready for mixing for the venison loaf. With all ingredients to hand, mix venison loaf ingredients as per the recipe and place in the oven. Turn your attention to the vegetarian curry and, while it is cooking (not forgetting to stir from time to time and add water if necessary), prepare the salad and drizzle olive oil for dressing,

PA=Purchased above in previous recipe

prepare the pineapple and place the chapatis on a plate ready to heat in the microwave (or wrap in tin foil if you prefer to cook them in the oven).

Once the curry is cooked, remove from heat and allow to stand until reheating just before serving. If you prefer to serve the curry straight away, heat the chapatis in the oven ten minutes before serving (or microwave for 2-3 minutes). Just before serving, break the eggs over the venison and grill (or bake) in the oven until the whites are firm.

LaVergne, TN USA
06 December 2010
2070LVUK00002BA